Journeys of a Child from the Village

Introduction

My name is Barry Christopher Archie. What's more important than who I am is where I come from. You may be (or should be) familiar with the phrase" It takes a village to raise a child"; well, I am a child from one of those types of villages. The village, which starts in my home (where all good villages start) is responsible for the person I am and the incredible life that I have lived, so far. This book is a collection of stories that comes from my journeys through life and how the village that raised me, prepared me for those journeys. All the names in my stories have been changed, one to protect the privacy of my family and friends (they don't want people knowing their business), two- to keep the focus on the purpose of this book, to bring attention to how those of us in the village (and yes we all are part of a village, like it or not), can affect another person's life, for good or bad. So, sit back, get a cup of coffee, tea, or whatever is your beverage of choice and prepare for a good laugh, or maybe even a good moment of reflection.

Table of Content

I Shall Fear No Evil

I am the seventh of eight children in my family, although this part of my journey takes place doing the time when there are only seven children in my family and I am the youngest child. I have always had a heightened sense of awareness for my age, which may be due to being a young child with a lot of brothers and sisters doing all sorts of things and exposing me to them along the way, or it may be due to my oldest sister.

My oldest (twelve years old to be exact) sister is very smart and loved being "the" big sister. I loved the fact that I could ask her anything about anything, and she would patiently give me full details about whatever I would ask her. At the age of four (yeah, I remember back that far), my sister made me feel I could do anything or be anything if I worked hard in school and made good grades. Boy, I couldn't wait to start! When I was five, all my other brothers and sisters were in school. They would all come home from school, take off their school clothes, and before they could do anything else, everyone would sit at the kitchen table and do their homework. I couldn't wait until it would be my time to sit at the kitchen table and to do my homework! To get in practice, I would often get my coloring book, crayons, and sit at the kitchen table with the rest of my siblings.

*One of my sisters, the one that is only eleven months older, would complain that "he is not in school, so he can't have any homework, and should be __removed__ from the sacred kitchen table"! My oldest sister (doing what was her regular duty of babysitting) told **my forever aggravating sister** (I say that with love) "no, let him do his homework". Fast forward about one year, which seemed like ten to me at the time, and it was finally here. Next Monday I would be* *starting school! I remember getting up at 4:00 am in the morning and getting ready for school. I think I should stop here to explain that my elementary school was literally located in my backyard, and the school didn't start until 8:00 a.m.*

My dad was up because he always had to leave about 4:30 a.m. to get to work. Dad asked me, "what you doing up so early Bo-Bo"? Bo-Bo was my dad's nickname for me. I told him, with all the excitement in my voice that a lottery winner would have, "I am starting school today dad"!!!! Dad smiled because he already knew the answer to his question, and I think he just loved the fact that I was that hyped about school. Heading out the door for work, dad stopped, gave me a hug, and said: "Have a great day son"! Soon after my dad left, my mom got up, and by this time I had gotten fully dressed, made my lunch, and was ready for the world. My mom looked at me with a look that was somewhere between "I am so impressed with my son", and "this boy is crazy"! Madear (this is what we called mom) said, with a pause in her voice, boy get yourself back in bed!! I went back to bed, but I kept my clothes on.

School was everything I dreamed it would be. Every day I was learning something new. I should pause here to tell you something else about myself, I had a speech impediment. Six years later I would learn that my speech impediment was due to me trying to talk at the speed of thought. As I told you earlier, I was the seventh child in a big family and had a heightened sense of awareness. This heightened sense cause me to start talking at the age of nine months! The problem with learning how to speak that early (as a very nice hearing technician would later tell us) is that the connection between speech and thought isn't completely developed. Thus, I would slur or mispronounce my words. It would be another six years until I would learn how to control this.

Another problem was that whenever I got nervous or scared, my speech would get worse. I also have to stop here and tell you about Romper-Room. Romper-Room was a room in a school where any child with any learning problem, be it physical or mental, would be placed in this room where basic daycare was given, and everyone from the kids who had to wear helmets, to the kids in walkers, and any other kid with any other perceived problem was placed in this room and kept separate from all the other children.

Okay, back to this story. As I was saying, I was loving school, but the school did not always love me. My first-grade teacher would get mad at me because sometimes she could not understand what I was saying. And of course, snapping at me just made it worst. I was sent to the guidance counselor. I had met this lady before and she did not like me or any other student! She would look at us the same way someone would look at a dead animal with maggots coming out of them. I said good morning to her once and she looked at me like "how dare is this maggot sprouting animal speak to me"? The guidance counselor had me sit at a table and told me she was going to show me ten cards and I was to say what was written on the cards. I think the guidance counselor spent about ten minutes with me. I didn't think about my visit with the guidance counselors until about two weeks later when my teacher gave me a red letter to take home with me to my parents.

A red letter was never a good thing. I remember it was a Friday and for some reason, my dad was off work. My mom and dad open the red letter together and read the last part of the letter out loud in the form of a question and were somewhat surprised, "your child is being moved to the learning focus class". I knew what that meant… Romper-Room!!!!! I spent the whole weekend in quiet terror. I saw in my mind every dream that I had dreamt of, before coming to school, dying.

My parents told me that my mom would be taking me to school Monday, and nothing else. Monday never came that fast in my life. My mom walked with me to school silently. My brother who was next to me in age (he believed he was my <u>real</u> big brother, although he was the youngest of my three big brothers) told me not to cry and that he would beat up anyone who teased me about being in Romper-Room. I had a knot in my throat from trying not to cry like my big brother told me, however, I wanted to beg my mother, "don't let them do this to me" but I was trying to be brave and I had to choose not to talk or not cry. I couldn't do both. When we got to school, the guidance counselor (who was now wearing a fake smile) escorted my mother and me to her office. In her office, was a very nicely dressed lady whom I had never seen before. My mother and I sat on one side of the table, and the guidance counselor and the nicely dressed lady sat on the other side of the table. The nicely dressed lady did all the talking. She had a

*very proper southern voice. She explained to my mother
how the change in my class, although appearing negative,
would benefit me in the long run. The nicely dressed,
proper southern voice lady then slid some forms over and
instructed my mother to where to sign.*

*My mother said "No"!! The nicely dressed, proper
southern voice lady said, "Pardon me"? My mother
repeated, "I said No", and then my mother reached into
her purse and pull out all my classwork and homework
assignments. My mother told the nicely dressed, proper
southern voice lady and the guidance counselor, "if my son
has some type of learning problem, then explain all the A's
and B's he has on his paper"? The nicely dressed, proper
southern voice lady looked at my papers with pure
amazement, and then she looked at the guidance counselor
as if she was waiting for some explanation for what she
was seeing.*

*However, before either of the ladies could speak,
my mother (using language that I wouldn't print, but would
love to) told the ladies that, "there is not a #@*##@*¥√∆
wrong with my son and if any of you #@*##@*¥√∆ do
anything to him I will come back up to this school and
#@*##@*¥√∆ every last one of you the #@*##@*¥√∆
up"!!! Then, my mom took my hand and said, "Let's go". I
started to cry on the way home. My mom looked down at
me and said, "don't cry baby, it's going to be okay". I
wasn't crying because I was still scared. I was crying
because these were the tears I had been holding in all
morning and because I looked up at my mother and
realized, "she is never going to let anything hurt me"!!!*

*I don't have the words to explain it the way I would
like to; I can only tell you that was the last time in my life
that I was ever afraid. I am talking about real fear, not a
ghost or things that go bump in the night. I am talking
about the fear that makes a person stop dreaming in life*

and work towards that dream; because you think someone can just come along and destroy you and your dream! I was taught in a church in my village about part of the 23 Psalms, the fourth verse, which says, "Yea, though I walk through the valley of the shadow of death, I will fear no evil…" I always remembered how on that day God showed up through my mom and taught me not to ever fear evil again.

Do You See What I See?

When I was young, one of my favorite times of the year was during the holidays. Even now (some fifty years later) the thought of the holiday from days gone by can create memories so vivid that I can actually smell the scents and taste the flavors of the foods that were cooked during that time. A road trip to my grandparent's home in Alabama was a regular part of our holiday tradition.

I don't recall my oldest sister and brother making the trip with us, however, I remember me and my other five siblings, making the trip, as well as a couple of aunts and uncles. We had this giant station wagon that held about twelve people, four in the front seat, four in the back seat, and four in the far back/storage area. I would always have a strategic plan that would allow me to be in the back seat of our giant station wagon. I loved to sit in the back because that was where the grown people sat, and I loved to hear the stories they would tell as they reminisce about their past; when they were young.

Listening, I would learn things about my parents that I had never heard before. For example, I learned that my mother was a star athlete, and was on her school basketball team. I also learned that my mother was a Sunday school teacher. My mother was a Sunday school teacher? Not to take you too far away from my story, but I have to explain that when I was young, the vision of the woman who could come up with curse words that were so complex to a point of genius, teaching Sunday school was like someone telling me that my mother could fly when she was a child.

I learned things about my father too! Things like he was <u>not</u> an athlete. In fact, he was the opposite, couldn't play any sport, not even just for fun. My father's talent was *in music. Even when he was young, he had a natural ear for music and could sing like a professional. Tells of my father as a child wasn't as surprising, because at that time he was the lead singer in the most popular gospel group in town, and I had always been told the stories about Sam Cook (a popular ex-gospel artist) coming to our home and trying to get dad to go on the road with him.*

Still, sitting in that back seat and hearing those stories was like being at the movies to me, and in the imagination of my mind, I could visualize everything I was hearing. However, there was one trip I especially remember. I was sitting in the back seat waiting to hear all the fun stories about my parents and the funny things they did as kids. Suddenly, as we pass by some type of landmark (the car was big, I was little, I couldn't see out of the windows) and my aunt said, "ooh child, remember when Mrs. What –you-call-them son was hung in that tree"! This revelation almost made my eyes pop out of my head. And then my mother chimed in and said, "yeah girl, and remember if you were caught after dark in such-and-such a place, they would kill you"! Once again, I was in a total state of shock, but there was much more to come. For what seemed like a week to me, although it was probably only an hour, I sat there and listen to tale after tale of injustice, unfairness, and all kinds of mistreatments that my parents, my uncle, and aunt had experienced growing up in this terrible, terrible place.

As always, my imagination was working overtime, seeing in my mind the video version of all the foul things that my parents and their family had suffered. I felt the knot in my throat tighten as I started to silently cry. And then, I hear something that completely and totally blew my mind; they were laughing!!! My mom, dad, uncle, and aunt were laughing, and not just laughing, they were laughing the way you laugh when something is really funny or something really good happens.

I went from sad to incredibly mad! WHAT WAS WRONG WITH THESE PEOPLE!!!!! I quietly thought to myself, for I had enough sense to know not to speak to my parents that way unless I wanted my mother to throw me out of the car while dad speeded up. My mom stopped laughing when she noticed I was crying, and she asked: "son, what's wrong with you"!? I wanted to explain to her that I thought it was the definition of stupidity to laugh at being treated so nastily and unfairly by people. Of course, I didn't say that. Otherwise, I wouldn't be alive now writing these stories. Instead, I chose a response that I felt was appropriate for the situation, "nothing"! My mom just shook her head and continues talking because I was always tearing up about something (that may have been due to that heightened awareness thing I talked about in the other story).

It would be about twelve years later (when I was about eighteen) that I understood what happened that day.

I came to realize that my mom, dad, uncle, and aunt didn't see what I saw. While in my imagination, I saw only hurt, pain, discrimination, and injustice. My mom, dad, uncle, and aunt look at the same scenes in their memories and they saw all of the things that God had brought them through. I then understood; they weren't laughing, they were rejoicing!!!

"It's Alive!!!"

Students will put ten times more energy in trying to distract a teacher from conducting class than the energy they used for studying. One day my students attempted this strategy on me, even though I had long before warned them that any trick they could think of, trying has-1.) I have already done it or 2.) I know someone who has already done it! Still, they try. So on this day that the class was scheduled to discuss the quantum-mechanical model of the atom, one of my students asked, "Sir, how did you become interested in science"? I started to call her on one of the oldest tricks in the book; get the teacher to reminisce about days gone by, and then I decided to go along with it.

*My oldest sister (my mother's second in command),
was a nursing school student when I was about five years
old. I loved looking through her biology books and asking a
thousand questions. My big sister loved the fact that I was
so interested in science, and would patiently answer every
question that I had. One day, I was reading my big sister's
book and came across a topic called "Artificial
Respiration". I asked, "What is artificial respiration used
for"? My big sister replied," when someone has stopped
breathing, like when someone has drowned, artificial
respiration is a procedure that can be used to help them
start breathing again". I had read about the scientific
method in my big sister's books and had learned how to
design and conduct an experiment.*

*So, I wrote an experiment to prove that artificial
respiration could be used to help lizards that had drowned,
to start breathing again. I can't remember exactly why I
choose lizards, except for the fact that there were*

thousands of them in the neighborhood. I recall gathering

about two dozen lizards, getting one of my dad's wash

buckets, filling it with water, and trying to drown the

lizards. I planned to drown the lizards and use a straw to

place them over their mouths and perform artificial

respiration. However, no matter how long I held the lizards

underwater, they would not drown!!! I tried all two dozen

lizards (boy I had extra free time back in those days) but I

was unsuccessful in drowning any of them.

So, I consulted with my big sister. I asked, "Why is

it so hard to drown a lizard"? Now I believe that almost

any other person that I would have asked that question

would probably reply with "why are you trying to drown

lizards"???? Not my big sister, for as I stated before she

loved the fact that I was so interested in science, so she

patiently explained that "lizards are amphibious". I, of

course, had a followed up question, "what does amphibious

mean"? Once again, my patient big sister replied, "that means they can live on land or in the water".

So, I left from the consultation of my big sister with the question in my mind, "what would make you drown if you are used to living in water"? Then, like a bolt of lightning, the answer came to me "pain"!! I got an old iron pot that my dad use to clean his tools, set up a makeshift fire source, and heated the water until it was boiling. I placed one dozen of my lizard subjects in the pot, and they all died. "Okay, the water can't be that hot". So back to the drawing board or pot in this instance, this time, I heated the water for fifteen minutes and tested it with six of the remaining lizards; they all die; the water was still too hot.

I repeated the procedure after ten minutes with two of the remaining lizards; they all died; still too hot. Once again, after five minutes and using three of the remaining lizards (don't know why, but I thought this would be it); all three died, which meant the water was still too hot. With my one remaining lizard, I carefully heated the water for one minute, and I carefully place my lizard in the water and…… eureka!!! The lizard did not die, with a pair of thongs (my big sister had some, don't know why) I was able to hold the lizard under the water and the pain of the hot water (I am sure it was pain based on the way the lizard was fanatically moving around) caused the lizard to drown. I pull the drowned lizard out of the hot water, placed him on the ground, and with the use of a straw perform artificial respiration, using the procedure as outlined in my big sister's biology book. I was so proud when the lizard coughed up some water and was revived. As a reward for being part of my experiment, I release the lizard back into the wild.

The students in my class had a wide range of expressions after hearing my story. In fact, I have noticed over the years (because this wasn't the first time I shared my baptism into the field of science) that the expressions of my students can be broken down by gender. Usually, the males in my class are satirically laughing or are staring at me with a joyful look of disbelief, as if to say "I can't believe you did that"!! The females in my class are sometimes in tears as they asked me, "How could you do that to those poor lizards"? Or, the females are staring at me with their mouths wide open, with a painful look of disbelief, as if to say, "How could you do that to those poor lizards'? After the flood of comments from my students, I joking reply," see that why I don't like to open myself up to you guys, you are so judgmental"! Then, I continued with my lesson on the quantum-mechanical model of the atom.

I Miss the Park

The thing about being in a big family is that you jockey for individual parent time. When I was five and the only non-school age child in the house, I enjoyed a once-a-month ritual with just me and my mom. Once a month, my mom would take me downtown on the bus to pay the gas, water, and electric bill at the city hall. This ritual provided me with many enjoyable privileges. I rode the city bus; I got a free balloon and a lollipop; I got to go to the city, and most importantly..... I got to have my mom all to myself!

The park became a symbol of private time for me and my mom. Mom would sit on a bench and I was given free rein of the park area. I played with everything and everyone. My mom would call me and I knew this incredible time was coming to an end; until next month. At last, all good things come to an end. I remember the last time my mom took me downtown to the park. The ritual was going, as usual, we rode the bus downtown, went to the city hall to pay the usual utility bills; I got my customary lollipop and balloon, and park time was underway. I was enjoying myself at full speed, and then I stop and got some water.

Now it is important that I explain that getting some water wasn't something I had done before, however, this day was hot and there was a bunch of kids in the park to play with. So, returning to what happened next; I was drinking the water from a water fountain in the park when all the sudden my mom came from behind me, grabbed me by the hand, and with a voice that indicated danger was near, she said, "let's go"!!!

We walked back to the bus stop, but at a pace just short of running. Once we were on the bus, my mother kept *looking out the side and back window of the bus. My mom's face wasn't showing fear; it was more like she was preparing to do battle. When we got off the bus we went home in a different direction and came in through the backyard. When we got into the house, my mom told me to go and play in my room. Now, once again, I have to stop and explain that back in the 60's parents made you go outside to play, and being sent to your room was a preamble to get a spanking. I asked, "mommy did I do something wrong"? She smiled lovingly at me and said: "no baby, you didn't do <u>anything</u> wrong, just go and play in your room, okay".*

Well, now I was really confused. I knew if I had done something wrong and my mom was mad at me, then she wouldn't have called me baby. Still, I didn't understand why I had been sent to my room? I listen through the door and heard my mom talking on the phone, and based on what I could hear, it sounds like she was talking to my dad.

My mom was saying, "no I didn't see anyone white at the park and I didn't see anyone following us on the bus……un hun,……… un hun….. Yeah, I got him in his room… no, we came home in a different direction… no, I didn't say anything to him…… Because I Don't Want To!!!!! "No, I am not taking it out on you…….. Yeah, I love you too…… it's going to be alright".

What had I done? I started to replay the entire day in my mind, from the moment that I woke up that morning, until the moment that my mom and I got back home. What had I done? I couldn't find an answer. Later, my dad came home; he came to my room and said, "How is it going Bo-Bo"? I started crying and told my dad that I had done something wrong, but I don't know what it was. My dad picks me up, hugged me, and said, "you didn't do anything wrong son, and your mom and I are not mad at you"!! My dad's voice calmed me, and he said for me not to worry and that everything would be ok. I was still confused about what I did or did not do, and why my mom and dad seem to be in a high state of alert. Then, my third oldest brother, the one closest to me in age, but believe he was my true big brother, came into the room. He asked me," you okay"? I say," yeah" (trying not to cry because my big brother was always telling me not to cry). I told my brother that I knew something was wrong, but mom and dad said I didn't do anything wrong.

Then, using a low voice that was totally out of his character, my big brother said, "I know you didn't mean to but you drank water out of the Whites Only fountain"!!! Now, I would like to tell you that at the age of five, I didn't know anything about Jim Crow or White Only signs, however, I did. My parents and all the people in my village knew that it was a matter of safety and survival for all the children in the village to know what those ugly words and signs meant. I thought for a minute and remember seeing the White Only sign out of the corner of my eyes, but I was

*having so much fun that I didn't notice it. I told my brother,
"so I did do something wrong", but before I could finish
my thought my big brother interjected, "No!! You didn't do
anything wrong, it's those signs and the stupid people who
put them up and the police that arrests you who are stupid
people"!! "Police", I quietly shouted, "I am going to
jail"? "Is mom going to jail"? My big brother quickly
assured me that no one was going to jail, but that is why
mom brought us home through the back road, and why she
didn't want me outside playing, so that if someone was
looking for us then they couldn't find where we lived. My
big brother also pointed out that if someone was coming,
then they would have already come.*

*That was one long night, however, nothing happens.
Soon after, life went back to usual until the next first of the
month. I don't know how I knew it was the first of the
month, the time of our bill-paying odyssey, but I did. I came
into the kitchen and saw mom putting checks inside some*

envelopes. I asked (hopefully), "mom, are we going downtown to pay the bills"? Mom said, "No, I think from now on I will just mail them". I said okay and asked if I could go outside and play; mom said, "Sure, go ahead. I went outside under the pecan tree that dad had planted the day I was born (he was always bragging about that) and just started to cry.

I wasn't crying for the miss bus ride, or the free lollipop, or the free balloon. I was crying because the park and all it symbolizes to me (my private time with mom) were gone. I didn't want mom to see me crying, because I didn't want her to feel bad or know that I had learned what happen that day. I felt that the least I could do is to let her go on if just for a little while, thinking that she had shielded me from the hate of the world. After about ten minutes later, I went on and started to play. Still and even up to today, I miss the park!

Get the Girl!!!

I don't remember the exact day. All I recalled was that sometime after my 13th birthday....I wanted to get a girl. What I would do once I got one? Well, I hadn't thought that far, but I knew I wanted one. In my village, they had a way of comparing a young lady's entrance into puberty and a young gentleman's entrance into puberty. For a young lady, they explained it like this, "a young lady, puberty is like learning how to build a powerful race car! There are certain materials and new skill-sets that had to be learned and you had to be mindful of the consequences of not taking care of this wonderful machine". For a young man, they explained it like this, "a young man goes to bed one night and has the incredible dream about this race car! The young man wakes up with an almost insane desire to get this race car! Now, he doesn't know what to do or say to get the race car, and he doesn't know how to drive! But oh God, he wants that race car so bad he could die"! Okay, review that for some of you who may have forgotten how it was at the age to help you understand my next story.

It was July of 1972 and an event called, "The Soul Festival" was being held at our state fairgrounds. Besides great soul music (those of you under the age of 55, go look up soul music), there would be girls there!!! My best friend, Dewayne Houser (not his real name), and I had been planning since March of that year for this festival. We knew our best chance of catching girls (boy that sounds terrible as I write it) was to go alone without any parental involvement. Our moms wouldn't be a problem, the problem would be my dad. My dad was a man ahead of his time, in that he was very protective of his baby boy (cannot tell you how much I hated it when he called me that back then). However, group events seemed to calm him down. So, Dewayne and I got five of our other friends to go in with us on the girl hunt (still sounds bad). Also, one of our friends had a sister who was six years older than us and was going to the festival also! 19 years old! That was a perfect age, old enough to impress a parent, young enough not to care a bit about us once we got to where we were going. So there, the plan was set and all I had to do was to present it to my dad. So, on the day of the festival (I didn't want to give him too much time to think about it), I gave my dad my perfectly rehearsed presentation, which I believe would guarantee me approval. Unfortunately, my dad had a better comeback by saying, "I got a better idea; you and Dewayne can just come with us since we are performing at the event and you guys can get in for free". THEY ARE PERFORMING AT THE EVENT!!!! You know there are times in your life when you are trying to figure out if God is mad at you or just has a weird sense of humor?

I have to stop here to give you a little background on my Dad. Besides working two jobs to provide for his family and being a deacon in the church, Dad was also the lead singer in one of the most popular gospel groups in the city. When I was younger, around 5or 6, I used to get up early Sunday morning to go with my Dad to the radio station to watch him and his group perform live. At the time, it was like being at Disney Land. Watching my Dad and his group in the recording studio with the station manager giving them hand signals to introduce the songs they were going to sing and timing them in to announce the different businesses that supported their program, as well as asking everyone listening to support those businesses, it all seems like magic to the six-year-old boy that I was at the time.

Okay, back to my story. I wanted to ask my Dad, "You do know that this is a SOUL MUSIC FESTIVAL right"? I also wanted to tell my Dad, "I appreciate your offer, but the worst thing you can do to find girls (that sounds a little better) is to show up at an event with your DAD"!! Nevertheless, all I said was, "Okay", with the best fake smile I could manage. I just didn't have it in me to hurt my Dad's feelings. I tried to sell the idea to my friend Dewayne. I explain that getting in free would leave us with more money that we could use to offer to pay for a young lady drink or something to eat! Dewayne looked at me with the expression, "You're kidding right". This followed by a look of, "Have you lost your mind"? After a few seconds of silence, Dewayne said, "Yeah, that's cool dude, but I think I'll just ride with the other guys as we planned". I said, "Alright", while trying to hide my feelings of betrayal, because deep inside if the shoe was on the other foot.... I would have chosen to ride with my other friends too.

So, we made it to the fairgrounds and some guy manning the back gate waves us through. I help my Dad take some of the sound equipment out of a van they had rented to the back of the stage and .....This is going to be just as bad as I feared it would be. The current band on the stage was jamming, and they had the crowd jamming with

*them. The band was playing a song that was one of the top
songs at the time and they sounded just like the record
(once again, if you are under 50, Google record). The
audience was standing on their feet with various alcoholic
drinks in their hand and they were JAMMING!! I started to
ask my Dad not to perform! If not for me, then for him and
his group, but my love and respect for my Pops wouldn't let
me do it. This, this was going to be a massacre!*

*After about four encores later, the jamming band
left the stage and an announcer told the crowd that there
would be a ten-minute break to allow the next group to set
up. My Dad asks me to give him a hand with setting up the
band equipment. I said yes, and why not. I was sure that
every good-looking girl had seen me backstage with the
group of guys who look like they had just come from
making a commercial for a funeral parlor! So, once my
Dad and his group started performing their Gospel Music*

at this SOUL MUSIC FESTIVAL, there would be no need

for me to ever try to get a girl again……..EVER!!!!

The announcer came to the front of the stage with a microphone and introduced my Dad's group, and included in his introduction that they were a GOSPEL GROUP. I knew it was wrong but at the time I felt I would hate that announcer for life. I looked out at the crowd from backstage and saw what I knew I would see. The people in the audience were staring at the stage the way deers do just before the car hits them. I even saw some of the people in the audience trying to hide the alcoholic drink that they were enjoying just minutes before. For a moment I started thinking about the priesthood and how old you had to be to join since it was clear to me that I would have to go through life without female companionship. Then, Dad came to the front of the stage. He introduced the group and himself to the audience, and then he said, "I know you came out today to get down with a little boogie-woogie, but with your permission, we would like to perform a little gospel for you this even. Would that be alright"? I don't know if it was the smooth way that Dad had said what he said or the kindness he always displayed in his eyes, but suddenly the audience stood up and cheered. Then, my Dad started to sing, " ♪ I found Jesus, yes I did and I'm glad ♪ ". The background singers, the piano player, the guitar player, the drummer, they all fled in place and my Dad and his group were JAMMING!!! The audience was jamming with them. People were standing in their seats and waving their alcoholic drinks in their hands. Right then I had a flashback when I was six, sitting in the radio station watching my Dad and his group perform. Then it just hit me, what was I thinking? My Dad and his group weren't some garage band that just got together from time to time. These guys were trained, professional musicians.

After what seemed like an hour of applause from the audience, the announcer came to the stage and said that there would be a 10-minute break before the last act would come to perform. My Dad asked if I would go to the concession stand and get some drinks for him and the group. Feeling an abundance of pride, I told my Dad, "Sure, no problem". I got 20 dollars from my Dad (he wouldn't be getting any change from this!) and off I went. While standing at the concession stand to make my purchase, three very nice-looking young ladies came up to me. First, I didn't say anything because I assume they were trying to get the attention of the person behind me, but then I turned to see....there was no one behind me! Then, one of the young ladies spoke, "Hi are you with the group that just performed"? Something or someone (until today, I am not sure which) told me to take it slow, don't show that you are excited that THREE GIRLS are purposely talking to you! Where were Dewayne and my other friends? What I *wouldn't give for them to see this. So with a cool voice, I replied, "Yes", then I turned my attention to the man working behind the concession stand and said, "Excuse me could I have four bottles of coke and two spites"? Another young lady asked, "Do you sang with them"? I replied, "No, not yet, but my Dad, **the lead singer**, has me in training to take over for him in a few years" (where that lie can from, I couldn't tell you). I once again turned my attention to the man working behind the concession stand and asked, "Oh yeah, can I also have two bags of Lay's chips"? No one had asked for Lay's chips, it just seems kind of cool not to focus too much on the young ladies and what they were saying. The last of the three young ladies wanted to know where would we be performing next. I told them, "We will be performing somewhere in New York, but we wouldn't*

know the exact date until our manager signs the deal for us" Now where did that gigantic lie come from? I truly couldn't tell you. My mouth was on autopilot and I was just letting it fly! I got my order from the concession and told the girls, "I wish I had more time the talk, but the guys were waiting on me". The GUYS were waiting for me? It like I said, autopilot. I cannot tell you how bad I wanted to just stay there and get every one of those girls' names and phone numbers, but something in me, some cooler advance part of me just took over. Still, I would have given away a kidney just to have had Dewayne and my friends see half of what just happened!

We loaded the equipment in the van my Dad's group had rented and headed home. During the ride home my Dad looks over at me and I had a smile bigger than the state of Texas. Dad said, "So son, did you have a good time"? I told him, "Dad, words.....I don't have the words". Later in my life, I learn that Dad had seen everything that happens at the concession stand. Still, for that whole day....I don't have the words!!!!

Fool's Gold

The importance and value of a good education were constantly taught to me in my village. As a teacher, I often wonder what happened to that message. Some have suggested that it's the price of integration and that with the new rights available to us (African-Americans) through the victories of the civil rights movement, African-Americans no longer need a quality education to live a comfortable lifestyle. Well, that's a bunch of crap! If anything, education is, even more, important when the people in a society have achieved rights and freedoms, so that those rights and freedoms cannot be taken away from them. The thought of this reminds me of when I learned just how important it is to have a quality education.

I was twelve years old and just starting a new school. I am going into the seventh grade! Middle School! To me, this was a major milestone, the next step to all the possible dreams I have had since the first grade. I remember the first day of school and walking the halls. I saw a series of big plaques with a big capital "A" on top. The plaques had students' names and labels titled - years and 1ˢᵗ nine weeks to 4ᵗʰ nine weeks. One of my teachers, my history teacher, was an African-American male.

This was special because African-American male teachers were starting to disappear in my school district, in fact, in my last three years of elementary school, there were none. I asked my history teacher, "What were the plaques on the wall at the entrance of the school? My history teacher said, "Each board represents a grade and a nine-week period of the school year." He added that "for each grade and for each year, they place the names of the students that made all 'A's during those nine weeks". Then he asked, why do you ask? Are you going to go for it? I thought for a minute, thinking how getting my name on that plaque who be a demonstration of my seriousness to be an outstanding student! "Yes", I exclaimed with excitement. My history teacher looked at me with pride and excitement, and then he said, "Cool if you do that you'll be the first African-American (well, he said black, I just like referring to myself as an African-American) student to get his name on the Honor Board"!

Well, that news motivated me even more. Not only would I have the opportunity to demonstrate my ability to learn at a higher level, in addition to that I could be a positive representation of my race. I remember how seeing my oldest brother work at studying so hard and how everyone in the village always remarks about how he was a positive role model. I was excited to think that I could be a positive role model for someone else. So, I went at it with full force. I didn't go outside to play after school, and all the free time I had during the weekend was all dedicated to studying.

Besides my history teacher, my other teachers had become aware of my goal and encouraged me to go for it. Every test, every quiz, and even extra credit assignments came back with a grade of "A", 100! At the end of the nine weeks, I was waiting for my report card like I waited to open a present at Christmas. When I open go my report card, and I very carefully open it, there it was; A, A, A, A, A, A, and A! I had made my first straight "A" report card. The school bus couldn't get me home fast enough, and it seemed to be a thousand hours before my parents got home from work. They didn't make it through the door before I jump up and yelled, "Look at my report card"!!!!! They were so proud of me, and that just made me feel like a million bucks.   Still, I had kept my goal of making the honor wall a secret. I had planned to tell them that they needed to come to school with me for something, and then,

Bam! I would show them my name on that honor wall and explain to them that I was the first African-American to make it on the wall. Now, I admit I never asked anyone what was the procedure for getting your name on the wall. I figured someone would give someone else my grades and that someone would have my name put on the wall. A week after we got our report cards, I came to school and saw the new names on the honor wall. I looked for mine, thinking it would be toward the tops since they were done in alphabetical order, but my name wasn't up there!

I asked all my teachers, including my African-American male history teacher, "why my name was not on the A honor wall"? No one had an answer, and I couldn't help notice how everyone seems so nervous when I asked them that question. The next day at school, while in my second-period reading class, someone came to my class with a note from the guidance counselor that said I need to come to their office. I wasn't sure why I was summoned, but I hope it had something to do with my name being missing from the A honor wall.

When I got to the guidance counselor's office, the guidance counselor started by asking me a lot of questions that appeared to be designed for putting off giving bad news. She said, "Hi, how are you doing today"? "Fine, " I replied. "That's great, that's great", she said, smiling so hard that I thought her face would crack at any minute. "Well, I guess you are wondering why I asked you here". "No, I don't"! Actually, I did. One of the many things you learn growing up in a village is body language. The village taught you that a person may be able to control what they say, but the face is a mirror of the soul.

So, as this guidance counselor presented her thesis on the difference in the learning levels of classes, and how the classes I took were at a lower level than the students who got their name on the honor roll plaques on the wall, I just sat there and listen. During this explanation, the guidance counselor's face looked as though someone was sticking her with a knife in the back. She was trying to maintain a smile, however, it was plain to see the lack of conviction she had with what she was saying. So, when she finished, I asked, "if that's the requirement, then why is it that three white students, all of whom took the same classes that I did and made all A's, names were on the honor wall plaque'? The guidance counselor's eyes teared up, and with a sad and soft voice replied, "I don't know"! I felt kind of bad because of what I had said... I just made that up.

However, as I said before, I had been taught that the face is the mirror of the soul, and I could see that the counselor was lying. After giving her a few seconds to pull it together, I asked if I could go back to class. With her hands still wiping away tears, the guidance counselor murmured, "yes". As I was walking back to class, I remembered someone in my village telling me, "You can lie to everyone except yourself and God". When I returned to my class, the teacher was looking at me as if she was trying to estimate the amount of damage that had been caused by a really bad car wreck.

With a voice set at a volume to encourage a positive response, my teacher asked me, "Is everything okay"? The response I wanted to give was, "Hell No! Everything is not okay, I am still living in a country that tells its' children if you work hard in life, you can achieve anything, however, I forgot to notice the little footnote to that glorious statement, which apparently reads, this doesn't apply to you if you are black"!!!!!!!!!! Instead, I gave my teacher the answer she was really requesting: "Yes".

My anger towards the whole situation didn't hit me until I went to my history class with my African-American male teacher. When I entered the classroom, he also asked: "Are you okay"? However, his question had an echo of pain behind it, and his face had a look of "I know you just been through Hell" all over it. Yet, I was angrier at him than any of my other teachers. I guess I felt that if anyone should have stood up for me, then it should have been him. To tell the truth, I don't know if my African-American male history teacher did anything to support me, although I learned many years later that my teacher had just started teaching, and the first three years that you start teaching you are on an "annual contract". Which means at the end of the school year you can be fired without any reason. I also learned that this young (although at the age of 12 he seems old) teacher had a wife and children. Yet, I expected him to sacrifice everything to stand up for me!

So, to express my anger I acted like a jerk the entire class. The teacher would ask a question, and without raising my hand, which was a class rule, I would make some type of stupid reply that made the class laugh. To my surprise, my teacher simply ignored me. He just continued teaching as if he was unable to see or hear me. At the end of class, my teacher called me over saying "Mr…… may I speak to you for a minute"? I walk over knowing what was coming next. I just knew I was going to get the- life is not fair and you got to keep your head up speak. Instead, this young teacher got straight in my face.

The expression on my teacher's face wasn't anger, it was much more intense than that. It was the type of look you would get from someone after you have pushed the button that released a bomb capable of killing an entire generation of people. With a low, strong, and intense voice, my teacher told me," you just got a taste of what it is like when life is not fair, and now you have an important decision to make; you can allow it to strengthen you or destroy you…. The choice is yours"!!!! Then, he instructed me to go to my next class.

I wanted to be mad at my African-American male teacher. I wanted to have a great big pity party, and complain about how this man, who did nothing to help me, was so mean to me at a time when everyone around me was mistreating me. I wanted to act out and respond to him in some nasty, disrespectful way, but in the village, you are taught that "when you hear the truth, your soul will know it"! So, as much as a part of me wanted to be hurt and mad at my teacher, I knew the words he spoke were the truth.

This all occurred on a Friday, and when I got home the village news network had already made it to my home. My mom was getting ready to go to work, but she stopped to ask me about the honor roll wall at school. As I said before, I hadn't told my parents about the honor wall. I planned to make an excuse for them to come to the school and I was going to surprise them with it. I told my mom that it wasn't a big deal and that it was only the 8th graders' names that went on the wall. I hated lying to my mom, but I saw how hard she and dad worked, not to mention all they had on them from having eight kids to raise, and at that time I just didn't want to give her one more thing to worry about.

You know years later, I learned that my mom knew I was lying, and she didn't push the issue because she knew I was trying to learn to deal with unfairness in life. I remember that during the weekend while watching TV, I saw a show about fool's gold. The man on the television show was going on about how Fool's gold, called iron pyrite, looks like real gold, but it had none of the properties or the value of real gold. You are often told by the people in the village that "if you carefully look and listen, then God will supply the answers to your questions, even if you don't know what to ask".

So, as I sat there in front of the T.V., my mind started to replay and evaluate everything that had recently happened to me, the conversation with my African-American male history teacher, and the program I had just watched. I realize that even though the school didn't give me the recognition I deserved, they knew and I knew that I earned the right to have my name on that honor roll wall! I also realized that the knowledge I had gained could never be taken away from me. In short, I met the challenge of my African-American male history teacher; I chose to be strengthened. A year later, the honor roll wall was dismantled!

"No... I Don't Do Love Her"

A lot of time what we learn in the village comes more from what we see than what we are told. When I was in the ninth grade, two of my brother's friends (that's my youngest big brother) were very much in love. I would often see them holding hands, kissing, or just looking lovingly into one another eyes. I wasn't the only person who admired their relationship. I would often overhear people saying how beautiful their relationship was. And then, the special couple went off to separate colleges and when they came back together.... All hell broke loose.

I can't remember what type of event we were at but I remember it was the first time that the special couple had gotten together since they had returned home and it was like watching a really bad car wreck.... in slow motion. I watched and listen in horror as the young couple whose relationship I admired was torn to pieces. She accused him of cheating, and he accused her, and they both cursed at each other so badly that no one could believe that just six months prior they were holding hands and constantly saying how much they loved one another.

Although I wasn't directly involved in that relationship, my heart was crushed! The fantasy of finding that special someone, your soul mate, was burned down a little more and more with each curse word that I hear the "loving couple" throw at one another. So, I decided right there and then that I would not have a steady girlfriend when I graduated from school! Fast forward three years and my senior year in high school were finally here.

I had taken every advanced class that I could take to prepare me for college, so this was my year to do something I always wanted to do: join the chorus. As I mention before, I come from a musical family. My father was a talented singer with a natural ear for music and all of my brothers and sisters had terrific voices. Music was just something that my family did, and I wanted the opportunity to perform in public.

Joining the school chorus was not as smooth as I thought it would be. Most of the members of my school chorus had been members for the entire four years, and even though my audition was flawless, the charter members didn't believe I had earned my place in the upper echelons of vocal royalty. Nevertheless, our chorus director admitted me in, and after doing a solo performance at the district level..... And winning, I was accepted by the other chorus members.

*The people in the village would always say,
"Everyone gets fifteen minutes of fame". Well, I think I got
an extra ten minutes. After the success of my district
performance got around, I became a mini-celebrity, and all
the sudden girls, who years before, had thought I was a
nerd for taking books home to study (I still don't get that
one), acting as though we were long lost, lovers! I held the
opinion that I was the same person then as I was when they
thought I was a nerd, so I gave a non-verbal "No thank
you" to their attention.*

*As I mentioned before, I had taken all my required
courses, as well as all of the available advanced courses,
so to take up the time I helped the choir director with the
junior chorus. The choir director asked me to help him
organize a performance group for the regional competition.
The group included this girl with the most beautiful brown
eyes. I think it's okay for me to admit it now (I mean it's*

been 37 years) that I purposely change the group partner assignments so that she would be singing with me.

However, I didn't think this girl had any interest in me; I would speak to her but she never spoke back. One of my friends in the junior chorus explained to me that the girl's parents were a doctor and a lawyer, and didn't want her dating anything but white boys! I would later learn that my friend was lying because he liked the same girl. It is okay, all is fair in love and war, and the guy ended up being one of the groomsmen at my wedding.

Anyway, getting back to my story, I began following this girl to her class trying to get her to talk to me, but no matter how many jokes I told or questions I asked she just looked at me like I was some crazy person. So, I decided to let it go. I didn't know why I was so obsessed with this girl in the first place, and yet there was something about her that I couldn't explain, not even to myself. All I knew was I felt as though I should be with her.

The people in the village would always say that God has a person for each of us and that all we have to do is be ourselves so that chosen person can recognize us. Since I was a kid, I wanted a family. I had always had a vision of me and my wife sitting around watching television, laughing, and just having a good time. For some reason that I couldn't (and still cannot) explain, why I felt this girl was the one!

However, this girl didn't show any interest in me, and I started to think that's a good thing. Did I forget my plan? I was going to go off to college unattached, without the possibility of having an emotional meltdown. So the more I thought of it, yeah, it is a good thing that girl ignored me. Yeah, she was pretty, but she wasn't the only pretty girl I knew. So, why couldn't I stop thinking about her?

One Saturday afternoon, I was just hanging out at home and all of a sudden the phone rang. I answered,

"Hello?" Now, this is back in the ancient days before caller Id or touch-tone phones. Anyway, no one said anything, so for verification, I repeated, "HELLO?" I was about to hang up the phone, and then I hear this small voice reply, "Hi". I thought I recognized the voice, but just to be sure I asked, "Who is this?" It was the girl from the junior chorus class that I couldn't stop thinking about and had decided to stop pursuing. I was so surprised to hear from her. We had a very short non-informative conversation. You know the one that goes like, "What are doing?" followed by, "Nothing, what are you doing?" The important thing was that I got the message that this girl was interested in me too!

So, what followed was the development of a deep romantic relationship. I hated it. I was doing the very thing that I promise myself that I wouldn't do. It wasn't the girl's fault. She wasn't chasing me, acting possessive, or anything that I could use as a reason to slow down or end our relationship. All I knew is that being with her felt natural! I was falling in love and there wasn't anything I could do about it. Nevertheless, I tried! I would talk to myself in the mirror, reminding myself of the terrible meltdown and destruction of romance that I had witnessed years before. I would leave home after the self-motivational speaks with the intent of breaking up, or, at least, slowing down our relationship, and then I would see those beautiful brown eyes and forget everything that I had just told myself! I was a mess. A sad and a happy mess.

I have been asked by numerous people, including my children, was the relationship that I had with this girl (who would later become my wife) love at first sight? The people in the village would say that love, at first sight, simply means that" This is God giving you the signal that you have a special opportunity to make something with this person", and sometimes both people have the foresight to recognize this and take advantage of it". Well, as I said before, I believe I have always had a heightened sense of awareness, however, this was the first time that this heightened sense worked against me.

So, I decided if I couldn't stop this then I will have the girl stop it. There was an after-school dance being held that Friday. I planned on taking the girl to the dance and doing something so stupid that it would make her break up with me. So, after having yet another counseling session with myself in the mirror (which I believe is proof that love is a state of insanity), I was ready to go and do what needed to be done. The dance was jumping and I was having a great time with my girl (Yea, I know I just referred to her as my girl! Shut up and just keep reading!). I asked her did she wanted something to drink. While on my way to get the drink, an opportunity presented itself. The music was playing and this other girl was dancing sooooo offbeat to it, so I started dancing offbeat to it as well. Soon, there was a crowd around us, laughing and cheering us on. The girl with the beautiful brown eyes came into the crowd, and looked at me as if to say, "What are you doing?" Suddenly, at the same time, something inside me asked the same question, "WHAT ARE YOU DOING?"

It was as if some future version of myself had popped into my mind to warn me that I was making the biggest mistake of my life!!!! So, after my little performance with that other girl, I decided to go to my girl and just come clean about all the things I was worried about. Just then, a romantic slow song had started playing, and I stood there across the room looking into my girl's eyes; this was perfect. I would go across the room, hold my girl in my arms and confess to everything. I have to stop here and point out why I know that God has a sense of humor. Just as I was making my move, this sexually dressed girl…… what girl you may ask; I didn't know (and until this day, still don't know) grabbed me and said, "Let's dance"! Before I could say anything, I looked up and saw the girl, the one I now knew without a doubt that I should be with,

walk out the out of the dance.

What do I do now? Part of me was wondering,

"What is your problem"? Isn't this what wanted? A bigger

part of me was wondering, "WHAT HAVE YOU DONE"?

And a smaller part of me was asking," God, why did you

wait until this time to send a sexually dress girl to me"? I

decided to just come clean. The way I saw it, I didn't have

anything to lose. So, I made, what seem to me, that long

drive to my girl's house. To my surprise, she allowed me to

come in. Once there, I started to explain the whole

scenario, about my fears of having a loving relationship

gone bad, and how I felt about feeling that we were meant

to be together. I couldn't believe how forgiving she was! In

the end, we agreed that at the end of my senior year, we

would end our formal exclusive relationship, and just

continue being friends. When the time came, we both

reneged on that agreement. By the way, on September 4th of this year (2014) we will be married for 31 years!

"You're Not Alone"

I love science. Always have. It helped to have my oldest sister, who was also interested in science, encouraging me to work and dream of being a scientist. There was only one problem. I didn't know anyone else who was African-American, and male, who shared my interest in science. I figured that once I got to high school there would be more people "like me" that would share my interest in science. Unfortunately, when I got to high school the situation got worse. Not only did I find myself the only African-American in my advanced science classes, but I was also constantly accused of "acting white' for taking those classes.

The support of my family prevented the accusations of "acting white" to deter me from my interest and pursuit of a career in science. On the other side, I had my fellow students and teachers of my science classes try to influence my behavior. The students would ask questions about my Afro (that was a hairstyle back in the '70s). They couldn't believe that a person who was truly interested in science would wear such a hairstyle. My science teachers would often question my choice of music, and suggest that classical music aided in concentration and comprehension of knowledge.

The people in the village would say, "If you don't teach your children who they are, then someone else will". My parents, along with my older brothers and sisters, made sure I knew who was and whose I was (a child of God). Without this knowledge, I can only wonder what would have become of me. Still, it would have been nice to have someone, who was like me, to share in my odyssey.

Fast-forward, I have graduated from high school and getting ready to start college. After looking at my scholastic options, I decided to do my first two years at the junior college (it is now referred to as a State college) in my city. I made that choice based on the calculation it would be cheaper, and all of the credits would transfer to ………State University. Filled with all the excitement and anxiety that comes with a new journey, my first day of college started with a stop at the student union. The student union of an educational institution is where all students, new and old, meet, greet, and just hype one another on.

I must admit, I was thrilled to see so many African-American male students!!! I was thinking to myself," Thank ya Jesus"! I wouldn't have to deal with being the only

African-American in any of my classes, especially my science classes. Two-thirds of the students in the student union were African-Americans (Yes, I counted), which meant I was ensured that I will no longer be the only African-American in my science class (Yes, I know I said this already). Finally, I wouldn't be alone.

So, with an "alright blood, I will see you in class", " goodbye", I went off to enjoy the first day of my first college science course. It took a couple of minutes to find the classroom. The room looks like it could whole about fifty students, and the class had been closed out because it was full. So, I sat there in my front-row seat, patiently waiting for the arrival of the following African-American, science-loving students. After five minutes, the classroom is full, and…….. I am the only African-American in the class! This cannot be real! I believed that I was part of some cosmic prank, and at any minute, some strange man will step out of a 4th-dimensional portal and announce,

*"Submitted for your approval, a young man who is confused with the environment around him. He has entered the twilight zone". This same scene repeated itself throughout the day and the week. I couldn't believe it, but I am **still** the only African-American in my science classes. So, where are the African-Americans? I found out that most were in Business school, some were in math. I had to accept it; I was doomed to be the only African-American in my science classes*

As disappointing as it was, the fact that I was used to my situation, made it easier for me to deal with it. Now, I am not suggesting that I was the only African-American taking science classes or had an interest in science, I just never came in contact with these other people. I didn't let my situation stop me, but I couldn't help thinking how nice it would be not to be the only one. I had to accept that this was my lot in life, and I would never be able to share my interest with someone who was like me or thought like me.

My oldest older brother was ten years my senior. So, while I was growing up I didn't have a close personal relationship with him. However, I did learn a lot from watching him. My oldest big brother acted a lot more mature than the other guys his age. He was very focused, and I believed if he hadn't been drafted into the military, he would have been the first person to graduate from college!

When I finish my first year of college, my brother and his family had just come back from being stationed in Germany. My brother and my sister-in-law were so proud of me, and the fact I was in college. They invited me to come and visit them in South Carolina. I felt honored that my brother was so proud of me, and I couldn't believe that he had invited me to come to visit him. As I said, my brother is ten years older than me, however, I didn't mention how I didn't think he liked me or my brothers and sisters who were closer to my age. I can remember all of us going to pick him up from some event. I would hear someone call his name and say, "Hey man, here comes the circus". My brother's friend (?) was referring to the fact that we were a big family and we packed a car like a bunch of circus clowns.

Looking back, I guess it was embarrassing for a 16-year-old guy, trying to impress girls, to have his family pull up in a station wagon full of kids. So, I didn't grow up thinking my brother cared that much for his younger brother and sisters. Therefore, I took this invitation to visit as a major milestone.

During my visit, my brother and I had time to talk, just him and me. I was astounded by the way my brother explained his positions on every topic we discuss. He had a clear explanation for what he was saying, he used vocabulary and reasoning that supported everything he said. Not only that, his sense of awareness of how what was happening in the world now had connections to things that had happened in the past, and could contribute to things in the future. He sounded just like………… me!

Hearing my brother talk was almost like listening to myself talk if I had more wisdom to go along with my intelligence. This guy was just like me, or I guess I should say that I was just like him. Why was I so surprised? I shouldn't be. We grew up in the same home, the same environment, the same village. We both had the love, support, and protection of parents. As well as, a big sister who offered additional support and unconditional love.

My brother and I could talk on, and on for hours until someone would come and interrupt us. It is still that way this very day! After that visit, I didn't only leave with a new connection and closeness to my oldest big brother, I no longer felt alone! I know that my brother was ten years my senior, and he wouldn't ever be in the same classes as me, nevertheless, just knowing that I wasn't the only one lifted some type of burden off me that I can't explain or describe.

All I know is since then, I don't feel alone in that part of my life. People in the village would often say that "The Lord will never forsake you are leave you alone". I now know that if I hadn't spent so much time complaining about what I didn't have, then I could have been more aware of what God had already given me.

The Awesome,

Enormous, Preeminent,

Power of...... Kindness.

My Dad was a quiet and happy person. He was always smiling, and he was always kind to people. This slightly dark-skinned guy was a country boy who was the eldest of eight children, which was a small family compared to the 15 or 18 kids norm for the farm community in which he and my mother grew up in.

Dad worked hard to get a job that offered more opportunities than the cotton sharecropper type future that awaited those who stayed in the Alabama town that he grew up in. Not only did dad get himself, his wife, and his children out of that dire lifestyle, but he also went back and got his brothers and sisters out as well. Dad was also the main person who went back and forth to check on his mother and father, right up until the time that they pass away.

You would think all the responsibilities of being the eldest son, as well as proving for a family of eight children and wife of his own, would make him a bitter and unhappy person; it didn't. I can only recall a couple of times in my entire life when my dad wasn't smiling and singing a song. My dad loved my mom, and he loved his children, all eight of us! Although he worked three jobs at one time to provide for us, all I can remember is my dad smiling.

As I said before, there are only a couple of times when I didn't see my dad smile or get along with someone. One of my older brothers had gotten in trouble with the law, and with my town and the small community that we lived in, everyone knew everyone else's business. We were in the barbershop, which was usually full of laughter and guy- talk when a guy who knew my dad came and said, "Hey dec (short for deacon), I hear about your kid getting into trouble with the law. Boy, I tell you, children like that just run a person down. I tell ya the truth dec if it was my kid..... I would just let him rot in jail". The entire barbershop came to a hush, and for the first time that I can remember the smile on my dad's face slowly disappeared. My dad stood up out of his seat, looked at the ill-mannered guy in his eyes, and said, "You're right if it was your son I would let him rot in jail too........ BUT THIS IS MY SON!!!!!"I thought for the first time in my long life (I was 10) my dad was going to get into a fight! However, before I could make a second thought, the guy who made the stupid statement said, "I am sorry dec, I let my mouth go off running without being connected to my brain". My dad, with his customary smile, returned to his face, replied, "Don't worry about, everything for love"

That was my dad. He was a kind and loving man. However, when I got older (in my teens), I started to resent my father's kind and loving nature, and at one point of stupidity, I thought it made him weak. Once when I was with my dad, he went through a bank drive-thru to make a deposit and to cash some checks. I should stop here and mention that drive-thru banking had just started. Anyway, dad was making his regular deposits, and in an attempt to be cute, the window cashier asked if I wanted a sucker? Yeah, right, I was 13 years old and most certainly did not want a sucker like some little kid (truth be told, I did eat it because it was butter rum, and I loved butter rum). My dad laughed because he knew I thought was growing up. So, *after receiving the deposit bag, my dad drove off. Later, we stopped at a convenience store to get something to drink. My dad opens the deposit bag and it contained about 15 bundles of $100 bills!!! To me, it looks like a million dollars. "Oh my God", were the words that came out of dad's mouth. My dad figured that the cashier, (who apparently spends more time coming up with ways to embarrass teenage boys than paying attention to her job) must have mistakenly given him the wrong bag!*

So what was normal for his kind character, my dad went back to the drive-thru to return the money. When he got up to the microphone, my dad whispered to the cashier that there was a problem with his deposit and he was going to send the deposit bag back through the chute. The cashier shouted, "No! Do not do that"! The cashier was looking at my dad as if he told her that he was there to rob the bank. The cashier quickly went on to say, "Sir, it is your responsibility to check your deposit before you leave the drive-thru, and if you later find a problem you would need to come back to the bank during regular bank hours (did I mention that this was on a Saturday) and fill out a corrective deposit form"!

Once again, my dad, being the kind, loving, and (crazy) patient person, tried to explain to the ticked-off cashier that the mistake was made by her. However, the cashier wasn't having any of it! I felt that this woman thought that my dad was trying to run a scam, and my dad did everything humanly possible to return the extra, extra, money; so let's go shopping! No, that just wasn't my dad. Dad just sat there, and let the cashier jump on her soapbox, and go on and on about the responsibilities of the customers before they leave the drive-thru. Once the cashier stopped talking (only to catch her breath) my dad held up the open the deposit bag and showed the cashier what he was talking about.

The cashier became very apologetic and continue to say just how sorry she was to my dad. Dad... well was dad. His only reply was, "Don't worry young lady, everything for love". I thought that Dad did everything humanly possible, and in return, this woman just got nasty with him. Today, I understand what my dad did, and even back then, a part of me understood. The village teaches you that anger is just a form of fear. The older I got, the more fearless my dad appeared to me. There are millions of memories I have of my dad's strengths, and one of them has to do with how, once again, my dad showed me the power of kindness.

I was all hyped up from being accepted to…….. State University. I had gone through new student orientation, put down a deposit for my dorm room, got my college wardrobe…. I was ready!! As I mentioned before, I had completed my first two years of college at home. Therefore, I would be going to……. State University as a 20-year-old adult.

About three weeks before school started, I got a letter that informed me, "Because we have not received your deposit, we regretfully have to inform you that your dormitory room reservation has been canceled". I HIT THE ROOF! I prided myself on keeping up my records and making sure my deadlines are kept. Plus, I had a copy of the canceled check that proved I paid my deposit. So, it is on!!

My dad overhears me discussing the situation with one of my sisters. I was telling her how I was going down to………… and get the hold thing straight! My dad says," Son, I am going to take off tomorrow and go to………… State University with you. I said ok. Now, I didn't want my dad to go with me, I mean am 20 years old and I knew how to handle my business. However, I loved my dad and I didn't want to hurt his feelings.

So, here we are on the road and I was riding with the conviction of righteousness, justice…. and my dad.

When we got to the housing office, I told my dad that I wanted to handle this situation myself, and if I didn't, then when would I learn to? My dad smiled and said, "Ok, just remember to be polite when asking your questions". I said yes sir, and we walked into the housing office. Behind the counter of the housing office, there was the young African-American sister who looked at me like I hadn't paid child support payments in the last six months. I walk up to the counter, and speaking as politely as could, I said, "Excuse me, I got this letter in the mail saying that I hadn't…………". Before I could complete my politely stated sentence, this she-devil from hell, snatched my letter out of my hand and started typing zealously on the computer. I started my internal cussing out countdown, "10, 9, 8, 7….. Before I could complete my countdown, my dad came behind me and put his hand on my shoulder. This delayed the countdown. The young spawn of –the –devil announced my dormitory room reservation was canceled due to the non-payment of the deposit. I am guessing

working for the devil doesn't come with a good vision plan

because my canceled check was stapled to the letter!

Just as I was about to explain how "reading is

fundamental", and how it was true that a "mind is a

terrible thing to waste", especially in the brain of someone

with enough activator in their hair to lubricate every rusty

nail in the state of Florida, my dad, using his soothing and

calming voice stepped in. "Sweetheart, could you check the

record using his last name first and his first name last"?

The young lady (my dad would want me to call her that)

reluctantly granted my dad's request. All of a sudden, the

young lady's whole attitude changed. She told my dad that

she would be right back. When the young lady came back,

she was joined by an older, more professional-looking

woman. The professional-looking woman looks over the

computer display, and then ask my father and me to come

to a room in the back of the office

Once in this back room, the professional-looking woman said that she would be taken care of the problem, and asked my father and me if we would like something to drink? My father said, "A little ice water would be fine, thank you". The professional-looking woman looked at me and asked, "What about you young man"? I wanted to ask for a bat or pole that I could use to beat the hell out of the young African-American girl who was so nasty to me when I first came into the office. Instead, I just said," Nothing, thank you". Which was dumb, because I was thirsty. People in the village would always warn that "Anger is like a hot rock....it burns the hands of the person who chooses to throw it first"

After about 30 minutes in the waiting room, another very pretty, professional-looking African-American woman came into the room and introduced herself as the director of student housing. The director told us that my dad was right about the housing department mixing up my name, and that is why my dorm room reservation was canceled.

The director also explains that "Unfortunately, all the

double-occupancy dorms had been rented out". Once

again, I started the curse you out countdown... 10, 9.8.....

Just then, the director told us that since this whole mix-up

was clearly the housing department's fault, she would give

me a private room at the double-occupancy price. Now,

even for 1979 dollars, this was an incredible deal because

a private dorm room cost about three times the price of a

double occupancy priced room!

As I look back at the times with my dad, I feel a

little bad that I ever thought that he was weak because of

his kindness. As I got older, I understood how kindness

doesn't only strengthen the person being kind, it can

change the people that you are kind to. I sometimes wish I

could go back and tell my dad how much I looked up to

him, how the love and kindness he always showed to

everyone was the greatest strength of all because it was an extension of the love and kindness of God! However, I

know he would just look at me and say, "That's okay son,

everything's for love"!

"And With This Ring"

I received my acceptance letter from the state

university on a Friday. I was so proud and felt this was the

final stage of my educational trek to becoming a doctor. I

had completed my first two years of college at my local

junior college, and I had taken the time to make sure that

all the credits that I had taken there would transfer. Matter

of fact, since I was told by the junior college's transfer

office, and confirmed by the state university's office, that all my credits would transfer, I decided to go to my junior college year-round to get as many credits as possible. The junior college tuition was much cheaper than the state university's tuition, therefore, I calculated that I would save a lot of money by taking as many credits as I could from the junior college.

When I attended the orientation for new students at the state university, I was disappointed to discover that although all my credits from my junior college did transfer, I still needed to take a minimum number of credits from the state university to graduate. I should have recognized this as an omen of things to come. I argued with the state university official about how I had checked with the state university office three times concerning this and no one told me anything about the minimum number of credits required for graduation. The state university official reply to me? "Oh well"!

It was 1979 when I started at the state university, and it was at this time that the country was involved in a major social change; Affirmative-Action. Many people felt that it mistreated those who were not members of a minority group. So, let me explain that the purpose of the Affirmative-Action law was to even the playing field by requiring employers and institutions, especially those who dealt with the state or federal government, to give **qualified** *minorities a fair opportunity to apply. In some of the worst cases, where intentional racism had been shown, the employers and institutions were required to have a minimum percentage of minorities in their organization. Reverse-discrimination suits and employers hiring unqualified minorities just to dispute the legitimacy of Affirmative Action was occurring everywhere. Now, I was aware of what was going on in the country because of Affirmative Action, however, I didn't think it had anything to do with me. I had worked hard for everything that I got,* *and the only thing that I ever asked for was a fair chance. I had no idea that I would be asking too much.*

Most of my professors were from the area of the sixties, and I wasn't prepared for the fact that most of them would act as though we were still in the sixties. I couldn't help but notice the change in their attitudes when I asked a question, compared to when other non-minority asked a question. At first, I tried to tell myself that I was just being sensitive. You are taught in the village that "when you think that someone is doing something to you…. Look at yourself". I had been given bad counseling concerning the number of hours I needed to take to be a pre-med major. I would later learn that no one should be taking 18 and 20 hours of classes per session. However, since I was the first in my family to go to college, I didn't know any better until much later.

Since my schedule had me taken the maximum number of classes, and I was working part-time to help pay for my expenses, I was living on four hours of sleep. I knew I was tired, which also made me initially question the perception of my professor's attitudes. Finally, I simply asked one of my professors why was it that when I asked a question in class I received some type of negative response in comparison to the other non-minority members of the class? Her reply was "Hum… I guess I do that"? That's when I realize that it wasn't me.

My entire two years at the state university were a constant battle. I went to the department office for help, and the required registration approval, but all I ever got was the encouragement to "hang in there". There was (and still is) an HBCU (Historically Black College and University) in the same city as my state university. Many of the African-American students who were in the same program as me, had already transferred to the HBCU. I didn't have any problem with the HBCU, and the only reason I had chosen the state university was that the pre-

med program I was interested in was stationed at the state university. I had resisted transferring because I felt it would be like quitting. Nevertheless, all my friends were encouraging me to transfer. I should stop here to mention that I hadn't spoken to my parents or any of my family members about my problems at the state university. I felt that I needed to handle this on my own. Bad call!!!

I remember going to the department office for my major and just asking what I would have to do to transfer to the HBCU. During my entire time at the state university, I never had anyone move so quickly and go out of their way to help me. The office personnel did not only get me the paperwork to complete the transfer, but they also gave me total and thorough instructions on how to complete it, and offered to submit it for me! I just stood there, looked at them, and walked out. I never went back.

All my classes were a struggle and I often had the thought of taking a break or just quitting school. However, the voices of my family were constantly ringing in my head. I could hear my youngest older brother saying "Get up boy, you aren't quitting"! I would hear my oldest sister saying" Come on little brother, you can do it"! The different voices of all my family members would flood my mind, and then in the image of my mind, I would see them. By them, I am referring to the little country boy and girl that raised me. In the imagination of my mind, I could see the hard dirt road they travel, the unjust world that they had to face every day, and the few tools and legal protections that life had given them to combat all the prejudice, unfairness, and dangers that they had to face. Yet, they didn't give up! These are the people who raised and love me and made sure that I had everything I needed to succeed. There was no way in Hell I could give up!!!!

So, for over two years, I worked, studied, and did everything I had to do to pass my classes, despite the uphill battle. I sometimes found myself in a ten-round bout with depression, asking myself, "What did I do wrong? I saw other students drinking and partying, while I lived on four hours of sleep, working and studying. It wasn't fair"! It was at these times that the voices of my family and the people from my village started to resonate in my mind and gave me the strength to push on.

I had made it to the last term of classes at the state university, and some changes were being put in place. For starters, we went from a semester system to a quarter system, and because of that, some classes that were required for graduation would only be offered once a year. Yes, you guessed it, I was in one of those classes.

My genetics lab was an open lab, which meant that it was open 24 hours to the students. The graduate student that ran the lab cheerfully explained to us that the lab was a requirement for graduation and that starting that year it would only be offered once a year. The lab used the cross-breeding of flies in our laboratory work. The graduate *student instructor joyously explained that if the generation of the flies that were given to us died, then we would be given an incomplete in the class and would have to wait until the following year to complete the class.*

The genetic lab was the only strenuous class I had left to do, and I was determined to do well in it because I knew that I couldn't do another year at the state university. I came to the genetics lab after leaving work one evening and the lab was locked!! I checked with campus security and asked if they could open the lab since it was already supposed to be open. The campus officer explained that they were asked by the biology department to lock the lab. The next day, I came by the genetic professor and the graduate student office to find out what was going on, and even though it was their office hours, no one was there. So, I went to the lab, hoping I would find the graduate instructor or the professor there, but all I found were other students collecting their samples of the flies. I asked my fellow students what was going on. They explained that the graduate student was in the laboratory earlier and told them that the lab would be closed at 5:00 pm every day from now on because someone had stolen a microscope.

Ok, let me stop here and explain why closing the lab early was such a big deal, and why the other students and I were taken flies home. In short, to use the files for cross-breeding, they had to be virgins, and you only have a short window after a fly change from the larva stage before it isn't a virgin anymore. I went to work at 3:00 pm every day, so if I didn't take my flies home, then I wouldn't be able to crossbreed them while they were virgins.

I took home my sample of flies and left them in my apartment so that I could work on them when I got off of work. I came home from work that evening and saw one of the most horrific sights of my life; the medium that my files were growing in had liquefied and my flies..........HAD DIED!!!!! Neither I nor any of my fellow students were told how heat-sensitive the flies' growth medium was, and why should they have, since we shouldn't have had to take the flies out of the lab.

Just the thought of having to stay at the state university for another year made my head throb with excruciating pain. What could I do? The only thing I could think of was to talk to the graduate instructor and try to work something out. Now, I blame myself for thinking that the graduate lab instructor would be understanding of the unfortunate situation that my fellow students and I had encountered. I pointed out to the graduate instructor that, "The genetic lab was supposed to be a 24-hour accessible lab, and if it was open then it wouldn't have been necessary for us to take the flies home, and they wouldn't have died"! The graduate instructor countered, "Well, if you or one of your classmates didn't steal a microscope, then we wouldn't have to lock the lab"! The graduate instructor went on to say, "Therefore, as you were told at the start of the course, you will receive an incomplete for the lab and have to wait until next fall quarter to retake and complete the course". There was no way I could stay at that university for another year. So, I responded to the graduate instructor, "Then I will sue"! The graduate instructor looked at me the way a king would look at one of his subjects after having them tell him to shut up, and then she replied, "I beg your pardon"! I replied," You heard me! I will sell everything I own and hire a lawyer"! I believe that the graduate instructor could tell by the look in my eyes that I wasn't bluffing. The instructor then said, "Well, I will talk to the professor over the program about what you said. Come back tomorrow and I will let you know what he says".

I came back to the genetic instructor's office the next day; hoping for the best, expecting the worst. The graduate instructor was waiting for me with a big smile on her face, and then she said, "The professor agreed to give *you another sample of flies and make the laboratory available to you 24 hours a day, however, he would not extend the deadline for you to turn in your laboratory report"! I looked at her for just a minute to make sure she was being serious, then I said, "The laboratory report that's supposed to be due in 27 hours"? The graduate instructor, still smiling like she just got away with murder, replied, "Yes"!*

Without seeing any other option, I agreed with the condition that I could handwrite the report. The graduate instructor agreed with the condition that I write in print and not cursive. So, I took off work for four days, got my fly samples, and went to work. It took me about 18 hours just to complete all the laboratory work and gather all my data. It was around the 22nd hour that I started to "hit the wall". Now, as I had mentioned before, I was accustomed to living on 4 hours of sleep. I had developed different routines that would help me stay awake, however, I had never had to go *this long without sleep. My hands were hurting so bad and had started blistering. My eyes were watering and everything I looked at was out of focus. Nothing that I could do was working! I thought about taking a quick nap, but I knew that if I laid down, then I wouldn't be able to get up in time to finish and turn my report in. I didn't know what to do, until I remember what I was taught by my family and my village, "When you are alone, you can always talk to God"!*

Now, what happened next isn't something that I have any proof of, or told a lot of people about. All I can do is tell you what happened. I didn't want to give up, and I wasn't worried about passing the course, I just didn't want to give up. I got down on my knees and prayed. I ask God for the strength to finish! I told God that felt if I gave up it would affect the people that came behind me, but mostly I just didn't want to quit! And then I got up off my knees and………. I wasn't tired!!!! It wasn't just not being tired, it was like I just got up from a 20-hour nap. Now, I will tell you the truth and say that it scared me a little at first, and then I thank God for hearing my prayer and went to work. Now, as I told you, in the beginning, I don't have any proof concerning what happened to me. I remember people in the village saying, "God will always allow you to see, but he doesn't make you look". I know all kinds of explanations that can be made up to explain what happens to me, however, I know what happens and I will never forget it!

I completed the laboratory report with about 30 minutes to get it to the genetic lab. I got to the genetics lab with 5 minutes to spare, and the graduate instructor was there at the door waiting. She said giggling, "I was just about to close the door". I respond with a straight face, "And I would have kicked it in"!! I would later learn that I made a B$^+$ on the assignment.

I went home for the weekend, something that I didn't usually do because I was always working. As I said before, I didn't even tell my mom and dad, or any of my family members about what I was going through, however, my mom and dad knew I was going through something. While I was at home, I got a letter from the state university. It was a form for the final payment for my college ring. Earlier doing the year, I had picked out a unique college ring. The ring had a "Tiger Eye" stone, and I felt it would represent "My determination to succeed". I sat there looking at the form, and thinking, "I cannot believe that I once had any respect for this institution"! The feeling I had for the state university at that time was below disrespect, it was somewhere much lower and much darker. I looked at that form for my ring and notice a warning that said if I didn't send in the final payment by a certain date, then my deposit would be forfeited. I remember thinking that they could take that deposit and choke on it!!! I took the form, thorn it into as many pieces as I could, and stuffed it into the trash can.

Before I knew it, it was here…. graduation day. My mom and dad, my youngest sister, and my girl (yes, we were still together) were all coming. I had paid for my cap and gown, as well as any other required fees to graduate. While alone in my apartment, a thought came to my mind, "You should moon them". I don't know where that thought came from at the time. I knew that the dark area attitude, somewhere way past disrespect, that I had developed towards the state university had grown solid in my heart and mind. It just made sense to me that these people know just how far down their mistreatment of me had taken me. I would later remember how the people in the village would warn that "The Devil is a liar, but he also uses the truth". It was the truth that made me susceptible to dark thoughts of mooning. I couldn't argue that these people deserved it, and maybe they would think twice before treating someone else like they had treated me! I should have known that Satin had something to do with what I was thinking because my last thought was not to tell anyone. After all, they would just try to talk me out of it. So, on graduation day there I was in line waiting to serve out my justice. Just as I was going on stage, I looked at the front row, and to my disbelief, there sat almost every instructor who had done some type of mistreatment towards me! I took this as a sign from God that what I had planned to do was just, and I wish I could induce myself to have diarrhea. As I was about to execute my form of naked justice, I caught the face of my mom and dad. There wasn't any type of assigned sitting, so I didn't have any idea of where my mom and dad were sitting. In their eyes, I saw so much! I saw the pride that can only come from a little country boy and girl who are now sitting in at university graduation, this is THEIR SON, which is walking across the stage to receive his diploma. The love coming from their smiles hit my heart so hard! It was like being struck by lightning! It took everything I had not to just burst out crying! And I forgot. I forgot about the instructors that had mistreated me, I forgot about the dark thoughts, pass disrespect that I had towards the university. All I could think about is the love of my parents, and how proud I was to represent them because I wasn't walking across that stage alone.....as always, they were walking with me!!!

About a month later, I was back at my parent's house looking for a job. I was feeling a little down because I hadn't found a job yet, and I realized that if I hadn't been caught up with fighting with the university I could have been spending time preparing and looking for a job. I would sometimes find myself having a relapse and starting to feel sorry for myself, but every time something would happen to boost me up. One day, a box came for me. The box was from the state university, and my first thought was something like, "What do they want now; a pint of blood"? I open the box and to my surprise…….. it was the graduation ring that I was going to buy! I didn't understand how I got it, and when I checked the packing slip it said, "Paid in Full". Then, I realize what must have happened..... My parents finish paying for my ring! I started to feel bad because I had torn that order form into as many pieces as could and stuffed it into the trash. I went to my mom and dad with tears in my eyes, I wanted to tell them how their love for me and the love from everyone in the family and our village gave me the strength to make it through everything I had overcome. I want to tell them that I realized that God was working through them to carry me through situations that I was unable to carry myself. I wanted to explain to them that if those people at the state university had the vision of divinity, they could have seen the enormous amount of love and protection that God had placed over me through them, and even more important, if I had taken the time to remember that, then I would never have been down or worried. I wanted to say all those things, but all that came out of my mouth, through a flood of tears was, "Thank you"!!!

My graduation ring turned into more than just a symbol of determination, it also serves as a reminder of God's love and the people that he used to reinforce that love, and I feel strong and loved every time I put it on!

Epilogue

Ok, so here I am at the end of my stories, for now. I would like to answer some of the questions you may have after reading my stories. Well, to start, mom and dad have gone home to heaven. I miss them with all my heart, however, when I start to feel bad I tell myself, "How can you feel bad? God bless you with two of the most wonderful parents that anyone could have, and it is not like they left me while I was still learning to stand on my own. I was almost 50 years old with my life on solid ground". Still, when I find myself facing hard decisions or just having a bad day, I can feel their arms around me.

Education-wise, well at the time of writing, I have gone on to receive a master's degree in science education, a Specialist degree in education, and a few months from now, I will receive my doctorate in science curriculum and instruction. Who knew that the little boy who loved science and had a speech impediment could go on to become an educator. I used the story of my challenges as an example for my students so that they can understand that no obstacle, physical or material, can stop you from reaching your goals.

The girl that I couldn't stop myself from pursuing, well at the time of this writing, we have been married for 37 years with two kids, a girl, and a boy. I am proud to say that both of our children are college graduates and that they are surrounded by a village of love, from us, their uncles, aunts, and a boatload of cousins. I remember

*daydreaming about having a family when I was little, and
although we have been through all types of ups and downs,
if it means that I would have my girl with me, I would do it
all over again.*

*All of my brothers and sisters are still with me, and
when we get together it is so wonderful!! We reminisce
about the little one bathroom house that we grew up in, and
how big that house seemed to us when we were growing up.
I think the main reason that the house looked so big was
that it was filled with so much love! Oh yeah, my youngest
big brother still thinks he is my real big brother!*

*As I look back at the life I lived so far, I am amazed
at how God has blessed, carried, and protected me. The
people in the village would often say, "The difference
between intelligence and wisdom, is that you have to live to
have wisdom! There are no shortcuts to it". I believe I have
gained wisdom from learning from the lessons that life has
taught me, and the biggest lesson that I learned is that*

everything is in God's hands; the good and the bad! I learned that if I trust in God, then I can trust that if I do everything that I am supposed to do, and it doesn't work out, then it was something that God didn't have planned for me. I learned that every hardship, every unfair experience, every plan that didn't work out, was just God's way of strengthening me for the next thing. These are hard lessons, but I can honestly say that the only time I missed out on something was when I didn't do what God told me to do.

There was a time when I was younger when I would beat myself up for what I did or didn't do. I learned that God even uses our mistakes to strengthen us. I remember one time when I was telling my oldest brother about my experience at the state university. I gave him a blow-by-blow description of the prejudice and unfairness that I experienced. My oldest brother just sat there and patiently listen to everything I had to say, and when I was finished, he told me something that I had never taken the time to realize. He simply said, "Yeah, little bro, but you made

it!!!" That one statement totally blew my mind. The people

in the village would tell you that, "When something

happens to you, you have a choice; you can be a victim or a

survivor. A victim is a position of weakness, and a survivor

is always in a position of strength".

Today, I am working to see myself as a survivor,

and I recognize the responsibility that comes with being a

survivor. I feel the responsibility to encourage others to

become survivors, or in other words, become a member of

*the **village**. You know it is funny, we all look for God to*

magically give us what we need, and he does give us what

we need; Each other!

So, I guess this is goodbye for right now. Thanks for

taking the time to read about my experiences in life, and I

hope that it helps or just makes you feel a little better about

your life experiences. I do believe that if you take the time

to look back at everything that God has brought you

through, then you will start to recognize how God has

blessed you too, and like my parents, myself, and the rest of

the people in my village, start to rejoice!!!